FOREWORD BY DARA CAPONIGRO
PHOTOGRAPHY BY SIMON UPTON

RIZZOLI
NEW YORK

New York · Paris · London · Milan

SIMPLICITY

NANCY BRAITHWAITE

TO
FOR
BECAUSE
OF
JIM

Authenticity. Clarity. Gutsiness.

Dara Caponigro

When I stand in a Nancy Braithwaite room, these are the words I think of first. Nancy creates havens of purity and calm. Frills fall away. Scale and proportion, air and light are all carefully calibrated. You get the sense that someone clear-eyed, honest, and committed has considered the environment with rigor. With an architect's eye, she manipulates space: expansive hallways that seem to increase square footage, pivoting walls that serve as doors, furniture she designs herself to exacting standards.

For Nancy, rigor is never synonymous with severity. She can find the poetry in something as ordinary as a simple white slipcover. I remember years ago, walking into her bedroom in Atlanta to find a wicker chair she had slipcovered in white linen and placed in front of a window. Sunlight flooded the room, outlining the ghostly shadow of the chair beneath the crisp fabric in a way that was surprising and astonishingly beautiful.

In my mind's eye I see countless other revelatory moments: a guest room in Atlanta with walls covered in hand-painted polka dots that could have so easily been hokey but in Nancy's rendering were just so damn chic. Or the wondrously pared-down kitchen in her vacation home on Kiawah Island, in which storage and every appliance, including the range, hide behind sliding doors. It sounds like it would be cold, but it isn't. Sunshine pours through floor-to-ceiling windows. There are warm, dusky stone floors, soft, honed- and wire-brushed granite counters, and two deep sinks in an island big enough for the whole family—husband, daughters, sons-in-law, grandchildren—to gather around and cook dinner.

That's the kind of designer Nancy has been for me—an eye-opening one. When we first got to know each other, in 1990, I was a young editor in my twenties, on staff at *House Beautiful*. The magazine had partnered with Nancy to produce a showhouse and we spent two weeks together, outfitting a new house soup to nuts. They were long, exhausting days, filled with conversation, laughter, and lengthy stylistic debates—over the color of a wall, the placement of a bed, the angle of the photographer's shot.

It was an education. Nancy is unflinching in her vision. No matter what style she's working in, she seeks always to strip things down to their barest, purest essentials. After the over-the-top, swag-and-jabot strewn interiors of the '80s, her approach was like a breath of fresh air. That goes for what she collected as well: Bill Traylor, Claude and François-Xavier Lalanne thirty years before they were covetable by every top designer. (Nancy abhors stuff for stuff's sake—she always strives for authenticity.) I came out of the experience with an appreciation for discernment that I hadn't had before and a new way of looking at the world, having absorbed the tenets of her sharp, sharp eye.

I also came away with a lifelong friend. As a person, Nancy has many of the same qualities as her interiors: integrity, honesty, humility. I think she's one of the great American designers of our day, but in an age in which an endless loop of tweets, posts, and feeds seems to inundate us with all manner of design personalities and ideas, Nancy is not a big self-promoter. She's content to go about her business, quietly pursuing her work. And for all her emphasis on strong lines and "power," as she likes to call it, she also has a reverence for the soulful and retains a wonderful sense of humor. This is a woman who isn't afraid to place a sweet stuffed animal on an otherwise angular canopy bed and who will treat the plainspoken beauty of a hand-woven basket with the same respect others reserve for fine art.

I've been photographing houses for more than twenty-five years and the funny thing about that experience is what comes to the forefront in retrospect. Everything but the truest things dissipate. When it seems you have seen it all, the really haunting spaces, the ones that stick with you after decades aren't necessarily the florid and dramatic showstoppers. Awe-inspiring rooms have their place of course, but awe isn't exactly the kind of thing one longs to come home to at the end of a harried, hectic day.

What you long for is peace. What you long for is simplicity. After twenty-five years of exposure to the best work out there, I've found that it's simplicity that's the hardest thing to do well. It is an art. And Nancy Braithwaite has perfected that art.

THERE IS
NOTHING SIMPLE
ABOUT SIMPLICITY

SIMPLICITY
IS COMPLEXITY

I see design in a very specific way.

My personal preference is for spaces that are strong and spare, minimalist yet luxurious, tightly focused but rich in visual pleasures, essential and without excess. I have a passion for interiors that transport, that captivate the senses, that envelop the viewer with a bit of wonderment. My goal as a designer is to create unique environments with clear, forceful identities—spaces that make strong visual statements. Every room should be comfortable, functional, and suitable, of course. I also believe deeply that the role of interior design is to command and fulfill the eye, not provide it with endless distractions. To be able to achieve this, I rely on something I call "simplicity."

I believe in simplicity. I also believe that there is nothing simple about it. Simplicity only occurs when every last element of a design solution strives to be essential, balanced, and powerful, with integrity, and no compromise in the details. It takes education, discipline, rigor, and skill to select what is suitable for a particular space, an individual client, and a preferred style. It is not easy to edit a world of almost limitless available choices, to pare away at what is possible to reveal what is absolutely necessary. Experience has taught me that the only way to achieve this is with an educated, principled, and disciplined eye. At the heart of this process, I think, lies the ability to see.

Seeing is a very difficult thing to do. Most people "look" at a lot of things but never "see" anything. Looking is emotional; seeing is an intellectual process.
—Albert Hadley

Designers have to be able to "see" critically. That means we have to know how to focus and touch, compare and contrast, in order to comprehend that "this" is not "the other," and evaluate when "this" belongs and "that" does not.

Without a trained eye, seeing that way is impossible.

Designers are visual people. Many of us are born with what people call "a good eye." We naturally seem to "see" form, proportion, and scale and understand the various relationships that make up a pleasing tableau or arrangement. But there is far more to seeing than that. Every good designer knows that he or she has to develop this innately appreciative eye into an educated instrument, one that can assess a vast array of visual information and distill it to its significant essence. That is what I call the technique of "seeing." It develops only with an eye that has studied, practiced, and evolved. This skill and comprehension, coupled with a uniquely individual use of visual information, is what I think truly distinguishes one designer from another. In other words, it is the informed point of view that makes a designer's style distinctive.

Learning how to see has been a lifelong process for me, both as a designer and as a collector. For my clients' homes and for my own, I work to identify, understand, and present the beautiful things I—and they—love and collect. I know how to use a purely decorative object for visual effect. My heart, however, lies with pieces that have integrity of form and substance and that meet a particular standard of excellence for their type. They seem to say, "Look at me, I am special." My duty as a designer, I feel, is to create environments that listen to the command of beauty, that treat each piece with the respect it deserves, and that allow each piece to achieve its full expression. My intention is to let every one of a room's components sing on its own—and also sing in harmony with every other facet of the given space, no matter how large or small.

Educating the eye to see critically takes dedicated work, intense and constant practice. It is the study of a lifetime, and I am still at it. Observing the surrounding world, taking interest and delight in its myriad components—these are the means that designers use to train our eyes. Curiosity and the desire for knowledge are essential to the process. For me, there has always been the imperative to seek out what is great, study why it is great, and learn how to put that information to practical use in the everyday. No matter the arena where I find it, excellence interests, teaches, and excites me. It always has. It always will.

Education seeks differentiation and nuance. At least, that is what education has proven to do for me. It obviously imparts essential in-formation—the facts, figures, and lore of history. It certainly introduces us to the hierarchy of knowledge and achievement. In my experience—which is still ongoing—educating the eye is a formative step on the path to being able to distinguish what is good, what is better, and what is best. The more we study and learn, the more we see and compare, the more we develop our own individual points of view, ways of assessing value, and personal sensibilities. Discernment and critical judgment follow in the wake of education and experience. Being able to sort through the options with clarity and understanding is absolutely essential to achieving simplicity. As we gradually grow confident in our ability to see, select, and edit, we continue to fine-tune our taste. Ultimately, we each arrive at a unique way of seeing and singular style that is ours and ours alone.

In the pursuit of simplicity I am guided by my principles. They derive from my education and experience, and they have proven to be the operating rules of each and every one of my endeavors. For me, the pursuit of excellence with attention to detail is first and foremost. I have a passion for searching out the best of everything. I need to touch items and understand them, so that I can weigh my choices against the highest standard in every aspect. Second, and probably most important, is my absolute respect for integrity, a constant in all things in my life. Third is to be as creative and innovative as possible. I love to think outside the box and approach the design process with an open mind. I often reevaluate traditional choices and expected solutions. These three principles, in combination, form the foundation of my approach to design, and over time have become my guiding disciplines. They serve me as I navigate through the many twists and turns of the problem-solving process that is design. With them, I endeavor to understand what can be best or ideal in the given situation. Then I evaluate the options. Only through rigorous application of my disciplines can I pare away and arrive at the necessary and essential. For me, this is the essence of simplicity.

As my eye has developed over the years, I have come to associate certain design techniques with my use of simplicity. I believe in building power in a composition by balancing strength against strength, whether composing an entire floor plan, a room, or just a tabletop. When I practice the discipline of subtraction, using three components in a space rather than ten, I must make sure that each of those three is far more consequential in its impact than any of the ten. In this process, I must consider the manipulation of scale and proportion, always a constant for me. I love overscale—and the clarity that comes with it. In my view, it can solve many problems. The repetition, duplication, and layering of forms also help to build visual authority and must be addressed. The juxtaposition of values within a unified color palette, be it pale or bold, can tie a room together so that it becomes more commanding. The use of texture, which I love, and the thoughtful use of pattern can then accent and amplify. Implementing these straightforward guidelines allows me to bring clarity of purpose to my work and express the visual and emotional strength that lies in simplicity.

Regardless of the decorative style or historical period, the effective impact of simplicity for me arises from the interaction of my fundamental design elements: commanding architecture, forceful composition, balanced proportion and scale, color, pattern, texture, craftsmanship, and frequently just the sheer beauty of form. When all are in synch, the effect is always forceful and often stunning. That is why I believe simplicity is opulent—and excess is not.

Early in my design career, a mentor, Richard Butler, introduced me to the idea of dividing design history, or rather, the furniture and objects that represent it, into three categories: country, classic, and contemporary. As a broad organizing tactic, this classification system has always stood me in good stead. Basic as it seems, this separation provides a useful way to sort through an overwhelming amount of material in order to get to the heart of what a given style means in the context of architecture and decoration. Further, my process of simplicity is equally applicable to each of these categories, as the projects and the way they are organized in this book reveal.

Country for me encompasses the many forms of design that are rooted in the practical demands of daily life in rural areas. Country forms tend to be crafted of materials close at hand. Often spare and unadorned, these pieces were intended to serve specific functions. Speaking first to utility, they frequently have beauty in their simplicity.

Classic, in my view, consists of the centuries of styles and the degrees of refinement that together form the great traditions. These are the looks that emerged from the palaces, vast estates, and great houses of the royal, the wealthy, and the well-traveled who commissioned trained designers and artisans to create one-of-a-kind pieces for specific settings. Crafted with luxurious materials, classic furnishings tend to be highly refined and ornamented.

Contemporary denotes a look of the time. It is a distilled, reinterpreted expression of traditional design. Based in the modernist, minimal approach to form and decoration, it is a style of clean lines and reduced ornamentation, innovative in form, function, and material.

I apply my principles of simplicity to every project I undertake, regardless of whether it is country, classic, or contemporary in style. Taking this principled approach as a beginning, my next step then is to assess and study the interaction of my fundamental design elements, which are the foundation of every interior I design. These components guide an interior's developing structure. They inform each and every choice and influence every detail. There is a definite hierarchy to the order in which I consider them. First comes architecture. Composition follows. Next are proportion and scale, and then color, pattern, texture, and craft. For me, interior design encompasses each of these elements on its own and, ultimately, in relation to all the others.

Each design element has its own body of knowledge that includes history, tradition, and an unlimited array of possibilities, some good, some better, some best. In striving for simplicity, the educated, principled, disciplined, and, of course, creative eye carefully and constantly evaluates each of these components and their interaction. Meanwhile, it is also engaging in the act of addition and subtraction to reveal the full potential and visual clarity, the magic and majesty that is simplicity.

Simplicity is the final achievement.
After one has played a vast
quantity of notes and more notes,
it is simplicity that emerges
as the crowning reward of art.
—Frédéric Chopin

MY ELEMENTS OF DESIGN

ARCHITECTURE

COMPOSITION

PROPORTION AND SCALE

COLOR

PATTERN

TEXTURE

CRAFTSMANSHIP

I've always believed that architecture
is more important than decoration.
Scale and proportion give everlasting
satisfaction that cannot be
achieved by only icing the cake.
—Billy Baldwin

Design at its best is often a collaborative venture.

I have been privileged to work with a number of highly accomplished architects over the years: James Choate, who designed our house on Kiawah; Norman Davenport Askins, who renovated our home in Atlanta; the Chicago architect Marvin Herman; Bobby McAlpine of Montgomery, Alabama; and Atlanta's Pak Heydt and Associates. On successful projects, the architect and designer learn from one another, support one another, and enhance each other's work. With the knowledge gained in the course of these collaborations, my appreciation and understanding of architecture has grown. I am deeply grateful to those who taught me.

Interior design can reinforce, complete, or haplessly negate architecture. At best, the two together make a living environment that is more appropriate, functional, and aesthetically pleasing than the sum of its individual parts. When the architecture is true and powerful, the designer's job becomes much easier.

Architecture for me is always the important beginning of each project. It is the sculptural skeleton. To analyze it, I consider function, proportion, scale, and aesthetic correctness. I explore whether it is necessary or possible to revise the architecture, or whether it is sufficient and does not need to be touched. Addition or elimination follows, if either or both are going to occur. It is at this point that I address the specifics of function in each particular room. I then use this information to develop a floor plan, which serves as the foundation of every other design decision with the understanding that the architecture is always primary.

OPPOSITE: This country room has powerful architecture components, tall vertical windows that allow light to flood into it, and a well-integrated fireplace as a focal point. Adding visual texture are high barn-wood ceilings and luxurious French limestone floors. All contribute to the success of this space despite a distinct sparseness of decoration. OVERLEAF: In much the same way, this country room with beam ceilings, antique floors, and well-detailed panel molding embodies the strength that architecture affords.

A dramatic and elegantly articulated classic staircase and railing
offer a bold example of how architecture can speak for itself.

ABOVE AND OPPOSITE: Supremacy of architecture holds forth in the contemporary ceiling. Scale, repetition, and pattern engage and delight the eye and give this room commanding presence.

For a house to be successful, the objects
in it must communicate with one another,
respond and balance one another.
—Andrée Putman

Composition is the arrangement of objects within a given space. This seemingly simple statement describes a process of design development that is actually quite complex and interactive.

Compositions inevitably occur within a set of spatial parameters; they vary from large to small. The largest composition is, of course, the architectural footprint. It consists of the placement and relationship of rooms within an interior, as well as the adjacent exterior spaces. This layout responds to the specificities of function and establishes the overall blueprint for the project.

Every room contains numerous compositions. Its floor plan is always the largest of these. Within the overall floor plan, there are many possibilities. They begin with larger seating arrangements and extend down to smaller objects on a mantel or tabletop. Some tableaux may consist of just one or two pieces; others contain many more. Each part of an individual composition must complement the other and enhance the group as a whole through harmonious interaction.

Countless compositional solutions exist to serve every functional and aesthetic need, though some arrangements are far more expected than others. Symmetry and asymmetry are two important overarching principles. Both are means to achieving balance and harmony. The interaction between the two can infuse a design with energy or throw it into confusion.

Repetition is one of my favorite devices. I consider it composition at its most straightforward. Repetition establishes an interior rhythm, directing the eye around and through a room in an orderly, measured way. It is also a useful tool for creating the illusion of architectural interest in a room where none exists. Groupings of like or similar objects always draw the eye. Duplication builds visual power.

Composition is also one of the many techniques a designer can use to achieve the unpredictable—that unexpected choice that so often makes a room memorable. Among the more obvious options is the selection and placement of an unusual object in such a way that the eye—and the emotions—take notice. Manipulation of forms within the room is a powerful means of generating surprise.

Most rooms, even the most serious rooms, benefit greatly from the inclusion of an unexpected touch—something deeply personal, imaginative, or nonchalant, something that expresses a flight of fancy or catches one unaware. Whimsy makes you smile. A smile creates a memory. To function at the highest level of design, that component of surprise—whatever it is—must be integral to the room's composition as well as to its style, context, and overall sensibility.

In this simply balanced country composition, a Southern American hunt board, a New England tiger-maple stool, and a European still life all reinforce and complement one another. The hand-painted and decorated wall completes the environment, adding patina and playfulness.

This country interior derives its success from the aggressive use of symmetry and repetition. Two matching chandeliers, four wing chairs, and a pair of identical sofas, all covered in textured linen, bring forth an unornamented but luxurious room.

LEFT: Unified palettes of color and pattern with carefully matched accessories highlighted with a tall bed as a focal point give verticality to this classic, low-ceilinged room. A quiet symmetry—what I call a sweet repeat—reigns. OVERLEAF: A classic room with almost perfectly matched furniture, fabrics, and accessories—and accent patterns of stripes and plaid—gets its strength from the use of purposeful pairing.

33

In the same contemporary room, an asymmetrical composition (RIGHT) balances a very symmetrical composition (OVERLEAF). These two arrangements, although opposite in principle, work together to draw the eye and achieve a balanced harmony.

The basic rules of proportion and
scale are unchanging. . . . The most
important element in decorating is
the relationship between objects—
in size, form, texture, color, and meaning.

—Eleanor McMillen Brown

Proportion and scale are intrinsic compositional factors and major tools in my lexicon of design solutions. The manipulation of either or both can drive the eventual success or failure of a room.

Proportion is the relationship of one part of an object to another. To the eye, a successful object usually has pleasing proportions, which are integral to its integrity. Scale, on the other hand, is the size of an object and its parts and its relationship to other objects and their parts. Comparisons in scale draw and compel the eye.

With proportion and scale, as with composition, I work from the grandest strokes to the most minute details. First, I consider the overall proportion and scale of the room itself, then its possible compositions large to small, and, finally, the individual objects that make up these arrangements. Large elements state their presence immediately and should be considered foremost; they set the footprint of the room. The more diminutive details then follow.

There are expected and unexpected ways to manipulate proportion and scale in a design equation. My preference is for the latter. The experienced eye knows how and when to defy the predictability of these. Increasing the scale of a design element to the anticipated proportions— and then pushing it beyond—carries with it the thrill of risk taking. It is an opportunity to put one's hard-won experience to work. I love to play with and subvert convention in pursuit of subtle, dramatic, and memorable solutions that can engender a sense of wonder. This is a goal I aim to achieve in each room and house I design.

OPPOSITE: An unusual, overscaled headboard design creates the opportunity for display. The proportional juxtaposition of the contemporary ceramics draws the eye, creating a focal point. OVERLEAF: Happily responding to one another in their grand scale, each of these country objects—pots, chairs, and eagle—is both complement and compliment.

PREVIOUS PAGES: Establishing the scale of this classic bedroom is a very tall leather bed, accompanied by silk Roman shades and floor-to-ceiling drapery panels. Completing and supporting the composition are appropriately scaled chairs, tables, lamps, and accessories. OPPOSITE: Large-scale columns and urns, manipulated in scale and proportion, create unexpected and dramatic architectural focus in this classic space. OVERLEAF: In this contemporary study, a boldly designed armoire with an inset plate of black porcelain forcefully states its presence and sets the tone for the room.

With color one obtains an energy that
seems to stem from witchcraft.

—Henri Matisse

Nothing in design is more mysterious, compelling, or personal than color. No two pairs of eyes are alike, so no two people see color the same way. Most important, the perception of color depends on the surrounding light. Because light changes constantly, color does, too. It is a capricious chameleon.

Like all elements of design, color can be functional. It can help disguise architectural flaws and redirect the eye. It can minimize or maximize spatial dimensions. Certain hues will seem to enlarge a space, while others will appear to make it smaller. Color may distract the eye from defects of line and form, poor proportion and scale. Lighter and darker values of the same hue, as well as the use of tone on tone, can build visual power where none exists.

Color has many aspects and can express different personalities. It may be pale and subtly ambiguous. It can be contemplatively complex and hold the viewer's attention as the brain tries to decipher precisely what the eye is seeing. It can be boldly energetic and invigorating, jolting the senses. In all of this, color can affect mood. Soothing or shocking, playful or serious, color is coy. It is constantly interacting with its neighbors and transforming through juxtaposition. Combined with pattern, texture, and finish, it changes qualities yet again.

Color should always be helpful, not hurtful. In my view, one should always choose color to support the design intent, whatever it may be. Most important, it is imperative that when making the color selection the designer takes into consideration the personal preferences of the client, the existing light conditions, and whether the room is intended for daytime or nighttime use.

Generally, for my eye, the more ethereal or complex the color, the greater its staying power and the better it fares in changing light conditions. That is true whether the tone is light, medium, or dark. As much as I love an all white room or a room in muted and ambiguous neutrals, I equally love a dramatic room of dark, velvety tones. A room saturated in a strong tone-on-tone palette can provide visual power, just as a small controlled explosion of color is always a simple and effective means of altering a moment.

So complex at all times, so ambiguous always—the potency and possibility of color is like nothing else in design.

The magic and mystery of color: using differing values of the same dusty, slightly ambiguous hue in various textures creates an atmosphere of captivating intrigue.

Contrasting with darkly aged woods and deep-toned walls are crisp whites that bring focus and attention to an intriguing corner of a country room.

ABOVE AND OPPOSITE: In a classic gentleman's study, red accents in silk and linen work like a dash of pepper to invigorate the design. OVERLEAF: In the classic dining room, shades of green inspired by the antique Zuber wallpaper envelop and surround the viewer.

Great blends of pattern, like great
dishes, must be carefully tasted.
And constant tasting is what
teaches a cook how to taste.
—Billy Baldwin

Pattern is a tool that a designer can apply purposefully or decoratively or both. The number of patterns available to a designer is endless, and it takes a learned and discerning eye to select the most apt pattern. To avoid visual noise, patterns need to be chosen carefully, mixed purposefully, and artfully applied. This takes practice and experience. Under no circumstances should a pattern overwhelm a room or its architecture, nor should it ever disguise the object to which it is applied. To do so negates its point.

For me, the most exciting use of pattern is purposeful. Functionally speaking, if a room is spatially challenged or lacking in verticality, pattern can help establish its dimensionality. If a room happens to lack a visual focus or is in need of visual jazz, pattern can provide that. A touch of pattern can draw attention to a room, a specific part of a room, or a particular object.

I love to exercise my imagination and be creative. When it is impossible to find a pattern that satisfies a particular need, whether decorative or functional, I can create one by cutting and pasting. That means taking parts of some patterns and combining them with parts of other patterns, thereby creating something new. This provides the client with a unique and personal design. That is the gift of pattern.

PREVIOUS PAGES: In this contemporary setting accented with Asian antiques, the use of a strong, subtle, and somewhat unexpected range of color allows the emphasis to remain on the furniture and accessories. OPPOSITE: Enlarged and with its colors inverted, the pattern of the Asian-inspired fabric on the chair and bolster becomes a woven border for an expansive custom rug in this classic room. In a purposeful blend, custom-designed bold striped draperies help to balance, enhance, and complement both the fabric and the rug.

For the walls of one of my country rooms, I designed a simple checkerboard pattern that is powerful in scale and color. As executed by painter Linda Ridings, it enriches, enlivens, and emboldens the space.

62

ABOVE: A traditionally inspired powder room displays a bit of whimsy. Walls covered with hand-painted scarabs bring a smile to a client in the pest-control business. OPPOSITE: The classic foyer has a striking black-and-greige checkerboard floor balanced by custom-made, boldly striped draperies and pillows. OVERLEAF: In an exciting use of purposeful pattern, walls with an elongated diamond design painted by hand bring dimensional verticality to this classic dining room; striped draperies mounted high under the crown molding further emphasize the room's height. Custom-made checkerboard pillows add a black-and-white accent.

A wall of broad horizontal stone stripes gives this contemporary bathroom a subtle yet dramatic pattern focus.

I search for the realness, the real feeling of
a subject, all the texture around it . . . I always
want to see the third dimension of something . . .
I want to come alive with the object.
—Andrew Wyeth

Every object, material, and work of art reveals an essential part of its character through its surface. Texture is the dimensional aspect of that surface. As such, texture is also a form of pattern, and that is how I frequently use it. In my view, controlled textural variety makes for an extremely interesting and powerful visual landscape—and a compellingly tactile one, as well. Above all, texture has great allure. It intrigues and draws the eye as it simultaneously invites the touch.

In interiors, texture comes from fabrics, woven and otherwise, but also from many other kinds of materials. Textiles can run the gamut from refined and diaphanous to gutsy and coarse, from simple and straightforward to intricate and complex. Most often my preference is for fabrics that have textures with great visual and tactile heft, but I am also equally fond of gauzy and transparent fabrics that filter light and can create an ethereal effect.

From walls, floors, and ceilings to furniture and accessories, everything in a room and in a composition has texture. Each component of the overall design provides an opportunity for the designer to introduce textures. With these come added interior dimensionality—a substitute for pattern, in my eyes.

That said, texture has its own set of rules for proper usage. Function, as always, comes first. I balance the use of texture with the intended purpose to make sure they complement one another. I also consider durability, practicality, and maintenance. Some situations require texture that can stand up to hard use; others do not. Often a gutsy and heavy texture, although visually strong, can be very fragile, and its application must be carefully considered.

I like texture and the extravagant use of many in one composition. As with pattern, I believe texture must enhance and reinforce, not distract from, the form onto which it placed.

The architecture establishes the textural envelope: a ceiling of antique beams and boards, antique wood floors, and hand-plastered walls with multiple coats of paint that create a patina. A sofa of hand-woven wicker with matelassé-covered cushions and nineteenth-century American chair with a woven rush seat complete the powerful textural composition.

In a mountain retreat in North Carolina, a tour de force of country textures incorporates a sisal rug, bamboo blinds, wicker chairs, and a burlap table skirt. The palette of fabrics and furnishings is rich in variety and lends a relaxed easy charm.

ABOVE AND OPPOSITE: With walls, draperies, and upholstery of custom-dyed silk velvet—one of the world's most extravagant fabrics—this extraordinary bedroom embraces classic, sumptuous elegance.

Natural textures, airy and lightweight, lend a palpable softness to a contemporary room. Chairs of abaca, open-weave linen draperies, and a hand-woven rug of multiple grasses give this beach house bedroom a cool, inviting air.

When a work lifts your spirits and
inspires bold and noble thoughts in you,
do not look for any other standard
to judge by: the work is good, the
product of a bold and noble craftsman.

—Jean de la Bruyere

A designer may have a unique vision, but turning that vision into reality often requires calling upon highly skilled craftspeople. As we work in concert, they provide us with inspiration and help to create magical effects.

Artisans of the highest caliber carry on the great decorative arts traditions and forge new paths. They are the keepers of custom and the enhancers of their craft. It is a gift to the designer to have the opportunity to work with superlative craftspeople in their fields—the cabinetmakers, the decorative painters, the metalworkers, the stonemasons, the weavers, the ceramicists, the upholsterers, the drapery makers, and the artisans in the fabric workrooms. Trained in age-old methods handed down from generation to generation, they often use their hard-won creative and technical facilities as the basis for innovation in form and ornament, materials, and production and construction methods. They always bring beauty, educate the eye, and create heroic singularity.

When a designer has the opportunity to commission a one-of-a-kind piece, there is a significant risk as well as great expectation. The pursuit begins with the vision. Then comes the journey of education and communication. The process of production follows. Finally, the fulfillment of collaboration arrives. If the craftsman and the designer have not communicated effectively, the creative process stalls. When the back-and-forth happens harmoniously, it is inspirational and exciting. The chemistry of collaboration is generative, and it makes for something remarkable, unique, and beyond what each involved in the creative partnership could have achieved singly.

OPPOSITE AND OVERLEAF: In 1850, a member of the Wood family of Nantucket signed the handle of this lightship basket, the smallest member of a nest of four, just as any artist signs his or her work. Highly prized by collectors today, especially when nesting and signed, these baskets were originally made in the nineteenth century on lightships, the vessels that served as floating lighthouses to guide ships through the dangerous shoals around Nantucket and safely into port. Stationed on these ships for long periods, sailors made the baskets for functional purposes, to alleviate boredom, and to supplement their incomes. These coveted baskets are still woven today, although on land rather than at sea.

Inspired by organic forms and by the history of
architectural ornament, the artist Robert Kuo has
reinterpreted both nature and the past in these
lotus blossoms. Hand-hammered of copper with a
silver-plated finish, they are classic and timeless.

This collection of sweet-grass baskets is by Mary Jackson, a master weaver. A fiber artist whose intricate pieces both preserve the centuries-old tradition of sweet-grass basketry and push it in astonishing new directions, Jackson received a MacArthur Fellowship (a so-called "genius grant") in 2008 for her contribution to craft.

COUNTRY

SIMPLICITY
WAS
BORN
FROM
NECESSITY

An American Story

Our house in Atlanta is a lesson in the history of American architecture, art, furniture, and objects—each with its own tale to tell. An American eagle, forty-two inches tall with a wingspan of five feet, proudly holds court in our sunroom. He is a masterful work in gilded tin, each feather hand cut, all with a shaded golden patina. He originally resided in an Ohio courthouse and dates to 1840. The artist is unknown. Quite by accident, we came upon him and could not believe what we had found! Discovering him was one of the highlights of our collecting career. He is a true work of American folk art.

Our home holds our collections of American antiques. We choose our pieces with the insight and approval of Deanne Deavours Levison, one of this country's foremost consultants in American antiquities. Deanne is, in fact, the guiding light of our collection and my dear lifelong friend. She and I met years ago, not long after my husband and I moved to Atlanta and began to collect. I searched for an expert in the field and found Deanne. While visiting her antique store, I was intrigued by a white swan decoy and I just had to have it! It was the first piece we purchased, and that marked the beginning of our collecting. That was thirty-five years ago.

When I met Deanne, she was acquiring pieces that were being sold to museums as well as to collectors. That intrigued me enormously. I thought if we were going to collect, we should be guided by an expert. Whether an object is of museum quality or not, it is essential as a collector to be able to evaluate what you see. The ability to perceive integrity in an object depends on knowledge and a keen eye. All pieces may not be museum worthy, but you still need to be able to judge their strengths and weaknesses.

I credit Deanne with teaching me how to see, not just to look. I also credit her with instilling in me an unwavering regard for integrity and authenticity. It was Deanne who introduced me to the world of great objects and taught me that these objects are great for a reason. She would show me an object, make me examine it closely, and probe me about what I saw. She taught me to see the purity in distinguished objects, to understand their form, to comprehend why they are beautiful, what their finishes reveal, and why and how that all works together to make a piece unique and a superior example of its type. If the intellect has been stimulated and the eye has been satisfied, the object is successful. Deanne also introduced me to Albert Sack's *Fine Points of Furniture: Early American*, one of the bibles of American antique dealers. Along with Deanne's tutelage, Sack's book led me to a major turning point in my understanding of the decorative arts. In the book, Sack posited that there are ideal forms and standards for judging an object to be either good, better, or best of its type. The clarity of those standards appealed to me enormously. The more we see and study, the more we refine our alertness and comprehension of an object's intrinsic worth. Not surprisingly, this aesthetic translates into design and decorating.

Our collection of American country pieces suits and enhances our American country home, which was originally designed in 1965 by the late James Means, a prominent twentieth-century architect in Atlanta. Means worked carefully to bring a sense of history to all the houses he designed. He based this house on the vernacular style of the New England farmhouse. At a time when everyone was in thrall with the new, he was repurposing elements of older buildings—paneling, timbers, floorboards—and incorporating them into his designs. Our house exemplifies this, as its beams, flooring, and roofing materials have been recycled.

With the help of architect Norman Davenport Askins and his office, as well as the landscape architect Bill Smith, the interior and exterior of this house have continued to evolve since we purchased it. I feel there is an important relationship between these two worlds. The plans for our home reside in the Atlanta History Center and represent a part of Atlanta's architectural history. Therefore, it has always been paramount to us to take Means's ideas and intent into consideration and to reinforce them as we expanded. Additions that stray from the original concepts often compromise the integrity of the original. We worked closely with Askins to develop proper continuity that is historically appropriate.

The house is traditional in its architecture, but departs some from tradition in its interior decorating—which, of course, is guided by my principles. I have designed each room for comfort, as well as to showcase my furniture designs and our collections. In each room, I have given great thought to composition, to the placement of each object. I continue to do so as my designs and our collections grow.

From the large custom-designed sofas to tables and chairs, the manipulation of proportion and scale is evident, setting the stage for objects to follow. Often we collect multiples of a category; these require space to breathe.

Colors run the gamut from light to dark, but are always filled with complexity and ambiguity. Throughout the house I have used tone-on-tone shades of white, dusty muted neutrals, and deep sueded shades for quiet cozy spaces. These colors envelop and calm. They also give a sense of continuity to the house.

There is a strong emphasis on texture and pattern everywhere, from hand-textured wall surfaces to ceilings with antique beams to rooms of antique paneling, as well as antique stone and wood floors. My love of linen is apparent, as the material is ubiquitous throughout these rooms. For me, the more dimensional the fabric, the better. Wall patterns abound. Early in my career, Douglas Funkhouser helped me to create the dots that appear on the cover of this book, as well as in one of our guest bedrooms. Jill Biskin, a highly accomplished decorative painter and my collaborator for many years, has developed one-of-a-kind, rather simple checkerboard, dot, and clover patterns that give our rooms a unique, quiet, yet powerful appearance.

Finally, there are touches of my love for the unexpected throughout the house and grounds. The François-Xavier Lalanne sheep in the courtyard are the most obviously surprising. More understated—but equally unexpected in effect—are the painted wall patterns, the textures everywhere, and the use of overscale furniture with pronounced verticality.

The hallmarks of this house are its sense of history, its comfort and livability, and the opportunity it has afforded us to preserve a bit of American heritage for our children and grandchildren.

PREVIOUS PAGES: In our front yard, Lalanne sheep welcome visitors as they approach the front of our New England-style farmhouse and its outbuildings.

PREVIOUS PAGES AND THIS SPREAD: With an eye to American history, hand-painted walls by Jill Biskin and eighteenth- and nineteenth-century crafted objects create a warm and inviting foyer. OVERLEAF: Embraced here, an American country setting employs American antiques in repetition, but without excess, and offers comfort via contemporary upholstered forms.

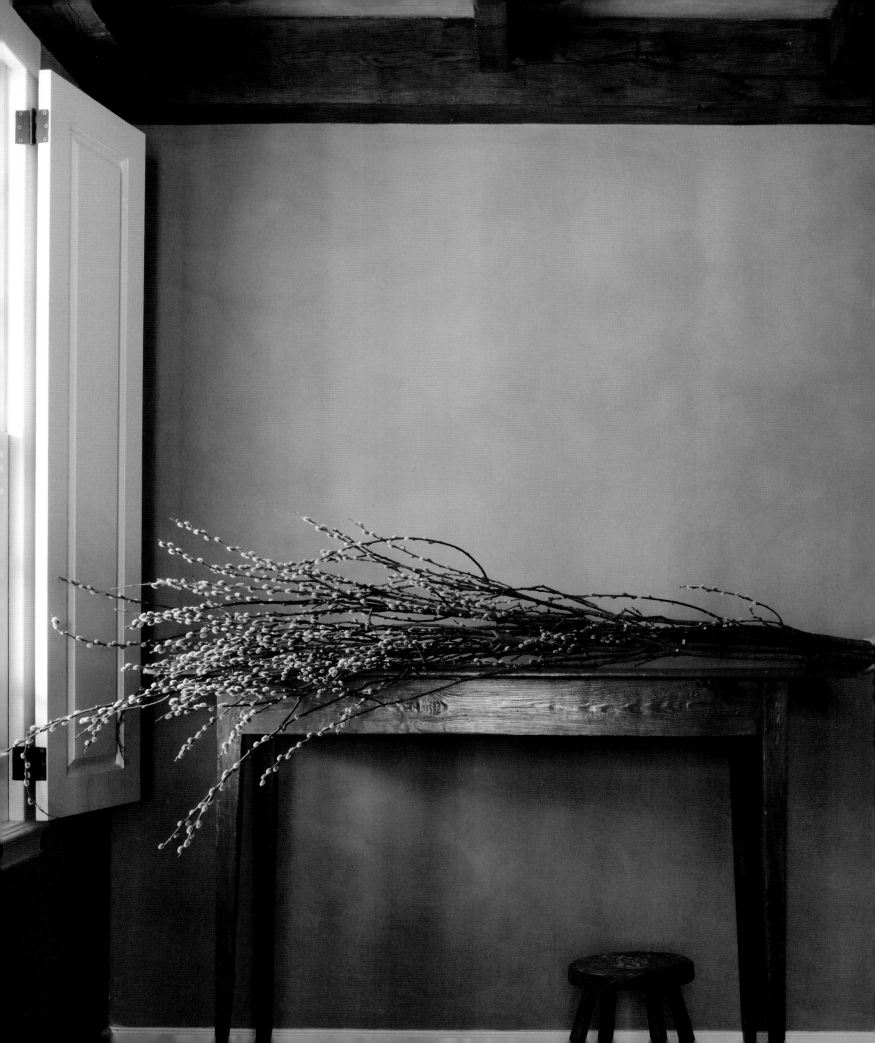

The Passion of Collecting

Deanne Deavours Levinson

Collecting, an adventure for a lifetime, can range from a purely decorative pursuit to an extremely serious endeavor. This is true whether the collector seeks to amass one single type of object or ranges widely across the spectrum of collectibles. It is also true whether the objects are antique or modern. The character of the collector is curious, passionate, and energetic. A collector is ecstatic with each acquisition and ever hungry for the next addition. Steadily, and almost invariably, the desire to expand one's knowledge about the collection ensues.

Whether antique or contemporary, each object has its own litany of criteria that qualify it as good, better, or best—or not. The collector and designer must learn about these criteria and train his or her eye in museums, with books, and with the help of experts. Where collecting is concerned, it is critically important to make knowledgeable choices.

The collector attempts always to acquire the best, and his knowledge of what is best is always widening. His is the task of judging between degrees of perfection.

—Arthur Davison Ficke

What makes an object great? The answer begins with its design: the integration of line, form, proportion, and scale. Just as with architecture, texture, and composition, integrity is the constant. The person who made the object had the eye and the technical skills to create a piece more successful from a design standpoint than those of his contemporaries. It also means that the object, if antique, was valued and respected enough over time that its original form or design has not been altered. If it retains the evidence of usage by those who have owned it over the years, its color and texture of finish only add to its appeal and value, both aesthetically and monetarily.

Collecting antiques means collecting history and learning history. These objects show us what they were, where they've been, how they were used. What remains reveals much about the life they've led. There is a unique and special enjoyment that comes with caring for things that have had a life before us and that will have a life after we are gone.

Collecting contemporary objects is equally exciting for someone who has this same thirst for artistic merit, but is looking for objects that speak to a much more recent time.

OPPOSITE: A form unique to the South, this tall slab bears amazing verticality and overhang. In its handcrafted simplicity, it is perfectly proportioned and aesthetically pleasing—a star in our collection. PAGE 109: Other prizes include a graduated set of antique burl bowls collected over the years that sit on an early sawbuck table with flanking benches, above which hangs a rare pair of wooden chandeliers. All of these pieces speak to the repetition I love and strive to achieve. PAGES 110-111: Close-ups reveal the table, bowls, and chandeliers in further detail.

Contemporary objects still have history, though, because from the moment an object is made, it is developing a history of its own. Because a collector's or designer's eye is trained to see, a collector or designer may discover great objects before the experts or the market. It's wonderful when that happens. The biggest thrill of all is when the market later proves that one's eye was right.

Ruthless, greedy, tyrannical, disreputable—
yet [collectors] have one principle worth all
the rest, the principle of delight.
—Kenneth Clark

The desire to collect something—anything—seems to be a universal trait, spanning all eras and locales. Without the long history of collecting, the world would be without great museums, galleries, libraries, and historic villages. The majority of the objects we view in those places are gifts from avid collectors who have become donors. Equally satisfying, however, is each person's simple pleasure and enjoyment of his or her own collection, whether large or small, antique or contemporary, Picassos or pebbles. Collecting is a love affair with objects.

Books are a hard-bound drug with no danger of
an overdose. I am the happy victim of books.
—Karl Lagerfeld

When Nancy Braithwaite first walked into my gallery in the late 1970s, she quietly walked around, simply looking. From my inventory of both high-style and country American decorative arts and European ceramics, she kept returning to a graceful swan decoy from North Carolina. Though neither of us knew it at that time, her eye was already leaning in the direction of simplicity, with all the composite elements she would later dissect and identify. The quiet, serene power of this spare swan form spoke to the visual principles she has continued to utilize throughout her career and collection. The bold construction of the sawbuck table, tall tapering legs of the slabs, fluency of the burl bowls, directness of the Bill Traylor drawings—all attest to Nancy's ability to glean fundamentals of design. It is then with the respect for the individual objects, personalization of their usage, and the composition of integration that makes this house and its collection distinct. It is calm and harmonious, exciting and whimsical. It is her personal taste, her sense of the spirit and soul of the objects, and her ability to make them communicate that permeate this collection. As with most collections, it is a happy, ongoing story.

Deanne

PREVIOUS PAGES AND OPPOSITE: The unexpected scale of a collection of New England miniature decoys happily swimming and flying across the mantel is an intriguing invitation to take a closer look. ABOVE: A crane of intertwined snakes lies in wait for the fire to be lit and the kettle to be brought.

The dining room is a composition of country, classic, and contemporary pieces. Mixing with Southern pottery and antiques are contemporary upholstered chairs, all boldly accented with a striped rug used as a table covering. A Japanese maple enlivens the setting, bringing in the outdoors.

In a simple, balanced composition, a seventeenth-century English Brewster armchair with amazing bold turnings enjoys the company of an antique Southern slab, a contemporary iron lantern, and Lalanne rooster clay pots. Although each is very different in style and period, with their individual strength, integrity, and contrast, they complement and support one another.

claude + françois Xavier lalanne

On a very cold day in the Clignancourt flea market in Paris, I discovered the work of the husband and wife team known as Les Lalanne: a small *pomme bouche*, or mouth apple, by Claude Lalanne and a large *mouton*, or sheep, by François-Xavier Lalanne. Although I was unfamiliar with their work, my eye quickly responded to these unexpected, pure, and straightforward forms. They exuded the kind of powerful simplicity in line that always inspires me. I was as completely taken with these pieces then as I am now. My husband and I made these discoveries years before the Lalannes' work became so highly prized. Today, their pieces are at home in the collections of such major institutions as the Cooper-Hewitt, National Design Museum in New York, the Centre Pompidou and the Muséum National d'Histoire Naturelle in Paris. In 2010, Les Arts Décoratifs in Paris organized a major Lalanne retrospective. A flock of Lalanne sheep along with many other Lalanne pieces took up residence on the meridian of Park Avenue in New York in 2009.

We have delighted in watching the renown of the Lalanne sculptures grow, even as we enjoy and appreciate those we live with every day. We have continued to collect their work. A wapiti, or elk, graces the jacket of the monograph *Lalanne(s)*, and another stands on our family room mantel. We have expanded our flock by adding two more sheep to the front courtyard. To the right you see a *coq* and a *poulet*—a rooster and a chicken—part of a brood that struts in and around our kitchen.

François-Xavier Lalanne, who passed away in 2008, turned to the animal kingdom for inspiration. He is quoted as saying, "The animal world constitutes the richest and most varied forms on the planet." Like Lalanne, I am amused, influenced, and energized by the animals that surround me—starting with the five cats who share our Atlanta home with us.

ABOVE: With its combination of fragile linen and sturdy wood, a rare burl bowl cheese strainer is an amazing example of a surviving late eighteenth-century utilitarian piece. OPPOSITE: The same bowl sits atop another example of endurance, a well-used Shaker cupboard with great verticality, unusual in that it was created as a stand-alone piece and not built in.

ABOVE, OPPOSITE, AND OVERLEAF: Early twentieth-century decoys are gracefully paired with pond grasses. Textured antique paneling and chairs lend themselves to this quietly harmonious natural setting.

THESE PAGES AND OVERLEAF: Designed as a vanity, this large, textured stone slab anchors the powder room. The addition of a contemporary glass bowl sink, which seems to float and almost disappear, brings focus to the eighteenth-century tinware sconces that line the walls.

PREVIOUS PAGES, ABOVE, AND OPPOSITE: Influenced by eighteenth-century designs, these walls painted by Douglas Funkhouser reinterpret an early form of wall decoration. The capricious and stimulating pattern has the look of age and patina. In contrast, it is paired with period wainscoting, floors, and furniture.

ABOVE AND OPPOSITE: In this house filled with traditions of the past, my grandchildren are beginning their own future traditions. Full of possibility and promise, they bring so much joy and creativity with them. Cats—both real and represented—have always been present and surely always will. In this guest bedroom, the large printed pillow is an antique German grain sack that complements the coarse, heavily textured linen that drapes the bed. The bed hangings are simply hung from cotton twine.

OPPOSITE: Lacquered round steel trays, polished stainless-steel walls, countertops, sinks, faucets, and lighting: contemporary forms and surfaces are present in a country New England house. OVERLEAF: A twenty-first-century kitchen housed in an eighteenth-century framework neatly hides refrigerators, ovens, and storage behind paneled doors, making this a minimalist, functional space, without clutter.

RIGHT: The kitchen offers a wonderful axial view into the sunroom. The doorway frames the marvelous gilded tin eagle from afar, enticing the viewer to enter. OVERLEAF: Unified in its color palette, with the repetition of furniture forms and the consistent use of heavy cream linen, the sunroom has a cohesiveness that spotlights the important work of Bill Traylor and allows the eagle to soar, just as it should.

RIGHT AND OVERLEAF: I designed a steel bar display system for our collection of Bill Traylor pictures that hangs from the crown molding and allows them to seemingly float in space. This unexpected relief from the wall gives them added dimensionality and enhanced importance. The Plexiglas boxes that frame them suit their straightforwardness.

Bill Traylor (signature)

Bill Traylor was born into slavery in 1854, in Benton, Alabama. When slavery ended, Traylor remained on the farm as a sharecropper. He raised his family, and cared for his animals. At age eighty-two, he moved to Montgomery, Alabama. There, he began to draw, creating both images pulled from his memories of living and working on the land and street scenes observed on Montgomery's Monroe Street. The artist Charles Shannon, who lived nearby, happened upon Traylor near a local blacksmith's shop, and for the next ten years he supported Traylor by supplying him with the materials and tools he needed to make his artwork. Traylor continued making art until his death at ninety-five, and today he is considered one of the most important self-taught American folk artists. He is often quoted as saying of his art, "It just came to me."

Traylor used materials he found at hand—cardboard, pencils, and paints—to make simple, direct images of people, places, and things. He articulated the rural concepts of his life with great vitality. He seems to have been able to render the essence of forms without any excess. This is something I greatly admire. With a certain kind of genius, and always with just a touch of naiveté, he interacted with and understood his surroundings.

The force of his simplicity draws me into his work. In my own design work, I also strive for power and simplicity. So much less can say so much more.

This early nineteenth-century North Carolina overmantel, a remarkable piece, retains its original painted surface intact. The repetition of the round form in the table as well as the bowls brings attention to the curves of the heart.

RIGHT AND OVERLEAF: François-Xavier Lalanne's petite wapiti graces the mantel. A bronze figure, monumentally simple in line and form, powerful without ornament or excess, it contrasts wonderfully with dark paneled walls and antique floors. It is the room's center of gravity.

THIS PAGE AND OPPOSITE: Jill Biskin's softly hand-sanded checkerboard on walls and ceiling adds a patinated surface that is impossible to achieve without the help of a great artisan. The finish gives this bedroom visual depth and warmth. The rectangular and square themes repeat in the bed, tables, and small cellaret at the bedside, reinforcing the room's geometric spirit. OVERLEAF: I designed this bed to incorporate bits and pieces of an eighteenth-century wainscot. The skilled cabinetmaker Bud Galland pieced together the many small parts and crafted a new crown and footboard, which Jill Biskin then masterfully antiqued to match the original finish. Freshly pressed white linen sheets and pillows create a contrast in luxury. PAGES 168-169: The sconces that encircle the entire room provide a quiet glow and highlight the wool that fills an exceptionally large antique wool gathering basket.

My dressing room (OPPOSITE) and bath (OVERLEAF) are cozy retreats appreciated at the beginning and end of the day. I love the welcoming light in the morning and use the blinds and sliding panels to provide privacy in the evening. A fanciful clover pattern on the bathroom walls repeats in the laser-cut stone floors. Matching faucets at either end of a very large tub allow me to choose my view of the garden from the window.

CLASSIC

SIMPLICITY
PARES
AWAY
THE
PREDICTABILITY
OF
TRADITION

Honoring History

When a grand house comes with a century or more of history and calls for renovation, it is imperative to consider the original architecture. This important New York townhouse, dating from 1895, had seen many changes over the years, most of them inaccurate. The previous owners had gloried in faux finishes, upholstered and mirrored walls, gilded cherubs, and over-elaborate moldings and ceiling paintings. That excess ornamentation diminished the rooms, which were impressive in scale and magnificently proportioned. Excited to reveal what survived of the original neoclassical details, I began scraping, sanding, and stripping. I pared away excess and revealed what was essential.

To establish an environment of luxurious serenity within the townhouse, I chose to concentrate on ethereal colors in pale-as-whisper shades. I selected Biedermeier furnishings for the spare, clean lines and the simplicity of the style. They formed quiet but elegant partnerships with the clients' collection of large-scale contemporary art, including canvases from Ross Bleckner and Jean-Michel Basquiat.

The materials throughout include heavy corded silks, taffetas, damasks, and mohairs. All add another layer of luxury. And this house, now in its present state of grace, speaks for itself.

OPPOSITE: The tranquil, sumptuous interior of this New York City townhouse pays homage to its early twentieth-century neoclassical architecture. Small and cozy conversation groups anchored by a soft linen velvet rug enhance the design of a room intended for entertaining. OVERLEAF: High ceilings, tall columns, and elegant moldings are all painted in the quietest monochromatic color scheme, accented by blackened floors so that there is nothing to compete with the architecture. Enhancing the Biedermeier and French forms throughout are the shine of silk and the flatness of wool damask and velvet. Paintings by Ross Bleckner and Jean-Michel Basquiat add modern highlights.

PREVIOUS PAGES: Dominating the marble and stone foyer is a commanding painting by Todd Murphy that all but covers the entire wall. The entrance, which is the size of two rooms, is a stunning exercise in the power of symmetry, scale, and duplication with matched pairs of Biedermeier stools, chairs, and settees. A pair of unmatched marble urns provides an unexpected accent. RIGHT: the billiard room, which functions as a home office, proudly supports a desk by the cabinetmaker Émile-Jacques Ruhlmann, a mirror by French architect and interior designer Emilio Terry, and a custom-made pool table. Walls, Roman shades, and draperies are all in highly textured chocolate wool mohair. A custom checkerboard wool rug and comfortable chairs upholstered in baby calf leather complete a private and restful retreat.

RIGHT AND OVERLEAF: Mid-century white chairs that once graced the Paris salon of couturier Marcel Rochas are playfully positioned in this master bedroom. Sumptuous velvet, taffeta, satin, and wool fabrics weave an opulent spell, while mirrored French candle sconces flank the bed to offer romantic night light.

A Collector's Penthouse

A client with an educated and articulate eye is unique. The privilege of creating a personal environment of the highest caliber for just such a client is something to which every interior designer aspires. In collaboration with the Chicago architect Marvin Herman, I was afforded just such an opportunity here. This client, as well as the architect, is a collector with a passion for and unerring discernment about objects and furnishings from the Art Deco, Biedermeier, and Wiener Werkstätte eras. Marvin and I worked closely together to create spaces that were architecturally appropriate and comfortable, that functioned flawlessly, and that presented the client's collections with merit.

Noble objects come with significant responsibility both to the client and to the designer. Sublime objects deserve the complement—and compliment—of furnishings that suit them in spirit and style, with the appropriate sensibility from the corresponding period(s). In pursuit of this perfection, throughout the design process I worked with a fine arts museum curator. Knowing how to find and identify an object that is best of its class is not easy. With the help of the curator I was able to locate pieces that were suitable for this residence and worthy of the client's collections. She and I focused on Art Deco and on the Wiener Werkstätte, a period that to my eye has a natural affinity with Art Deco. Our search took us to Vienna several times, and to Paris, to dealers renowned for expertise in their area of the market and their access to significant pieces in the given periods and styles. Our close collaboration proved to be a fascinating education and experience for me. Gradually, we assembled a superb array of one-of-a-kind pieces by Ruhlmann, Hoffmann, Subes, Danhauser, Sue et Mare, Chareau, and Daum, as well as by current day craftsman, including Pollaro and Linley of London.

To anchor and complement these collections were walls paneled in book-matched and hand-lacquered beech wood, custom-made upholstery, and luxurious fabrics that included silks, silk velvets, mohair, and calf leathers. In all of this, functionality and comfort reigned. The result created was a memorable kind of luxurious simplicity.

PREVIOUS PAGE: In the foyer of this residence, a pair of original Josef Hoffmann upholstered lounge chairs support the curve of the stair. OPPOSITE: Though petite in proportion and scale, a macassar ebony and ivory chiffonier and chairs designed by Art Deco master Émile-Jacques Ruhlmann have an outsized effect. They easily hold their own and command and demand attention in this small, high-ceilinged antechamber. OVERLEAF: Comfort and elegance hold court in this superbly appointed living room accessorized with masterful modern pieces by Ruhlmann and Pierre Chareau.

The dining room that adjoins the living room holds additional Ruhlmann pieces, including an impressively sized mirror hanging over a cabinet (ABOVE) and a superbly scaled Daum chandelier (OPPOSITE).

In the family room, a sublime Biedermeier oval desk by Josef Danhauser stands in stark contrast to stacked flat-screen televisions over the fireplace. OVERLEAF: Past and present are again juxtaposed in the form of important art works coupled with comfortable, functional banquette seating.

An apple a day? Yes, please. But the *Pomme Bouche* on this bedside table is special: it is by Claude Lalanne. This small guest bedroom is ultra-luxurious in the use of fabric: a heavy silk figured damask contrasts with the colorful sheen of satin and the sheer shimmer of the horizontally striped silk under-draperies.

Focus On Art

For the art collector, art affords an ever-changing conversation with the viewer. For this interaction to occur, the art must be displayed in an appropriate space. This client, a serious collector, imagined a home to house her extensive collection but also entertain her many friends, children, and grandchildren.

Art, of course, was primary in the development of the design scheme. Her collections included ancient as well as contemporary pieces, some diminutive and some larger scale. With holdings that span the Romans to the moderns and include expansive works on paper by such twentieth-century masters as Willem de Kooning, Jackson Pollack, Pablo Picasso, and Louise Bourgeois, the interior required sufficient wall surface to give each breathing room. The many smaller items in her collection, in contrast, needed settings that invited the observer in close.

In collaboration with architect Norman Askins, we developed the shell into a complete floor plan for a new spatial environment: a soaring, double-height, forty-foot-wide living room braced by a pair of smaller rooms, one for dining, the other, a library. Second-floor balconies in the living room bring the volume back in touch with human scale and provide additional areas for art display. Second-story windows provide indirect daylight. Because every piece was light-sensitive, lighting was of major concern. In particular, sunlight had to be controlled. With the help of a museum consultant, we placed and aimed artificial illumination precisely.

So as to not distract from the art, it was important to consider color, fabrics, and furnishings very carefully. To anchor spaces, her smaller existing French pieces needed to be reinforced by larger scaled pieces. Walls, moldings, and fabrics throughout were in neutral hues, in values medium to dark. This created a cool, quiet palette. The serenity of these spaces, in contrast with the gutsiness of the art, creates a certain tension. They act as a foil for each other, and reinforce each other, too.

PREVIOUS PAGE: A circular anteroom that welcomes and guides guests through the front door houses an intriguing, bronze cast-stone sculpture by Judith Shea that sets the stage for what follows. OPPOSITE AND OVERLEAF: In the art-filled foyer, a dramatic sweeping staircase and a palette of subtle dark hues highlight works by Willem de Kooning and Martin Puryear.

204

Panels of silk drapery enhance the verticality of the double-height living room and the oft-used library beyond.

A quiet spot in the living room brings focus to the third-century-B.C. limestone stele and a bronze sculpture by Gaston Lachaise. OVERLEAF: At the other end of the living room, a Robert Mangold painting and a Joel Shapiro bronze are surrounded by the client's French furniture collection.

Dominating a round dining table that accommodates the client's love of art and conversation is a steel-wire sculpture by Shi Zhongying.

215

A custom-made steel bed that rises to the ceiling artfully frames a gouache by Sigmar Polke.

CONTEMPORARY

SIMPLICITY
BEGINS
IN
TRADITION
AND
ENDS
IN
INNOVATION

Island Sanctuary

A proud *Quercus virginiana*—a live oak tree—graces our Kiawah home. Stately and grand, it is one hundred twenty-five years old and a specimen of its kind. Amazingly, it survived Hurricane Hugo without any structural damage. Just as amazingly, when we purchased the lot we were unaware that it existed at all. It was buried deep in the property, completely hidden by surrounding trees. Discovery of the tree marked the beginning of a highly creative, three-year collaboration with architect James Choate on the design of our vacation home in South Carolina. This powerful tree became the visual foundation for what was to follow.

Being the client for the first time was an exceptional experience. It afforded me the opportunity to put my own ideas, principles, and disciplines into practice and to make decisions based solely on the needs of our family. My goal was to build an innovative, powerful, and functionally comfortable home. The resulting contemporary structure stands tall to capture views of the Atlantic on one side and low country marsh on the other.

The house, like the tree, has an extremely forceful presence. Heroic in scale, with three forty-nine-foot vertical gabled pavilions, large expanses of windows, and vaulted eighteen-and-a-half-foot ceilings, it offers a sense of spaciousness and light. Minimal in décor, it has a serene spirit. Most of the rooms are comfortably intimate in size, but appear overscaled because of the soaring ceilings.

We intended the house to serve as a family home, which factored significantly into the development of its layout. My husband and I use it by ourselves, of course, but we also gather there with our two daughters, sons-in-law, and their young families. We worked with Choate to organize the floor plan around private areas for the three individual family units and large communal spaces for all. When it is full to capacity, the areas that provide privacy are important.

The first level houses four guest bedrooms. On entry there is a wonderful indoor/outdoor swimming pool that is just four feet deep for child safety purposes. The main living spaces are at the top of the house. The living, dining, and kitchen area runs for forty-seven feet along one side. On the other side, parallel to that space, are the master bedroom and a home office. Indoor/outdoor porches connect the two. From the porches, we enjoy listening to the sounds of the ocean waves and seeing the wonderful marshes filled with ducks and egrets. Running through the structure is a stair that reflects the structure's verticality: the first, exterior portion of the stair is massive; the interior stair is purposely light and airy, with open risers and very thin pickets doweled into the wood railing. The upper half of the stair turns so that as you approach that landing, the ocean comes into view.

As the kitchen, dining, and living areas are one communal and connected space, I wanted to conceal the kitchen when it is not in use. I designed eight eleven-foot-tall sliding doors that, when closed, appear to be walls and conceal refrigerators, ovens, cooktops, and storage. The kitchen consists of two workstations; they are mirror images of one another and can function separately. Our sons-in-law enjoy cooking and each likes to experiment in his own space. I decided on this double kitchen during the planning

phase; upon completion, I was pleased to discover that the system actually worked. A well-known chef cooked Sunday brunch in the kitchen after the wedding of one of our daughters. I asked timidly, "Does this function?" She said, "Yes, it absolutely does."

For me, it was important that the architecture and interior furnishings of this house work in concert. Powerful architecture demands and deserves this. The relatively small proportions of the majority of the rooms coupled with the vast verticality of their lofty ceilings and the large-scale stone slabs for walls and floors manipulate the perception of scale. By eliminating baseboards, moldings, and exposed hardware, we reduced the quantity of architectural detail, making properly sized furnishings even more important. Standard size furniture here would look as if it had been made for a dollhouse. To respond to the architecture, furniture and decorative objects needed to be overscale and therefore custom made.

This house is about craft. In contrast to our Atlanta home, it is about contemporary craft, the majority of which is based on historic tradition. We have collected and commissioned pieces from a remarkable group of artists and craftspeople. First and foremost is Mary Jackson, a master basket weaver and Mac-Arthur Fellow. Her sweet-grass basket, approximately forty-two inches in diameter, has a special place in our hearts. It was the inspiration for this house, as I wanted a piece that spoke of the area: sweet grass is native to the region and masses of it separate the back of our house from the marsh. Basket making is a traditional low country art form that has been passed from generation to generation, and it is one of the oldest types of African art in the United States. My husband and I have known Mary Jackson and her husband, Stoney Jackson, for more than twenty years, during which time we have become friends. I have great respect for her as a craftsperson. I honor her innovative creativity, which acknowledges but pushes traditional boundaries, her simplicity of line and form, and her ever-present integrity.

Also reinventing tradition is Chinese-American artist Robert Kuo. Kuo created the copper snails and toads, marble hares, lacquered fish, sheep, and rabbits that provide surprise and pleasure in this house. Working in many different materials and scales, he is inspired by organic forms as well as timeless Chinese decorative motifs. My first discovery, the sheep, instantly beguiled me and started me on the path to collecting his sculptures.

French sculptor and designer Christian Astuguevieille made a number of the furniture forms and objects here. Bounding with imagination, he creates completely unexpected pieces with heightened textural interest.

All of these artists—and their work—share the simplicity of line that my eye continually seeks and demands. They satisfy my love of innovative surface texture and whimsy. Working with these unique people and collecting their objects has been an ongoing exercise in pursuing forms that bear a certain essential clarity.

Building this house was an experience my husband and I embarked upon together. Yet, in essence, it is his gift to me. He believed in what I wanted to do and gave me a free hand to make it happen. I have used all of my abilities and experience to create a unique place for us and for our family, which, in turn, is my gift to him. My hope is that it will be handed down in our family from generation to generation.

PREVIOUS PAGES: The massive oak in the front yard sets the scale for the house and balances the architecture successfully. Repetitious and powerful like the house itself, the three chimneys embolden the composition. OPPOSITE: Huge stone steps introduce the house and connect the outside to the inside. ABOVE: Measuring five feet wide by eleven feet high, the pivoting glass and steel front door serves as a preface to the heroically scaled interiors. OVERLEAF: In the stone-paved foyer, a thirty-three-foot-long handwoven striped sisal rug, massive stone planters, and copper balls by Robert Kuo continue the vigorous proportions. PAGES 232-233: At a stone pool just beyond the foyer, enormous stone rabbits, also by Robert Kuo, add a playful note. PAGES 234-235: The foyer walls are painted to match the striped rug. Custom lighting by Kevin Reilly adds the appropriate finishing touch.

RIGHT: Robert Kuo's gigantic copper snails enjoy an ocean view as they slowly glide their way up a fifty-five-foot interior stone wall. OVERLEAF: One side of the house enjoys a sweeping view of the Atlantic Ocean. PAGES 240-241: On the ocean porch, Kuo's fanciful lacquered fish have found a home, and a flight of doves has paused momentarily to rest. PAGES 242-243: The hallway off the ocean porch leads to the dining space, which has as its focal point a massive stone fireplace. PAGES 244-245: A close view of the exotic, bi-colored ortegon leaves.

OPPOSITE: A massive, custom-designed steel and stone table comfortably seats eight people. OVERLEAF: African trays and a collection of wonderful ceramics and stoneware add pattern, power, and dimensionality to the dining room.

OPPOSITE: With expansive views of the Atlantic, the light-filled living room, carefully minimalist in décor, easily accommodates multiple families while remaining comfortable and functional. OVERLEAF: Balancing the exuberant textural strength and scale of Mary Jackson's sweet-grass basket are Christian Astuguevieille's woven rope drum stools, their effect amplified through repetition. The different forms are equally artful and innovative. PAGES 254-255: A close look at Christian Astuguevieille's furniture and sculpture reveals him to be an intriguing experimental artist whose forms abound with imagination.

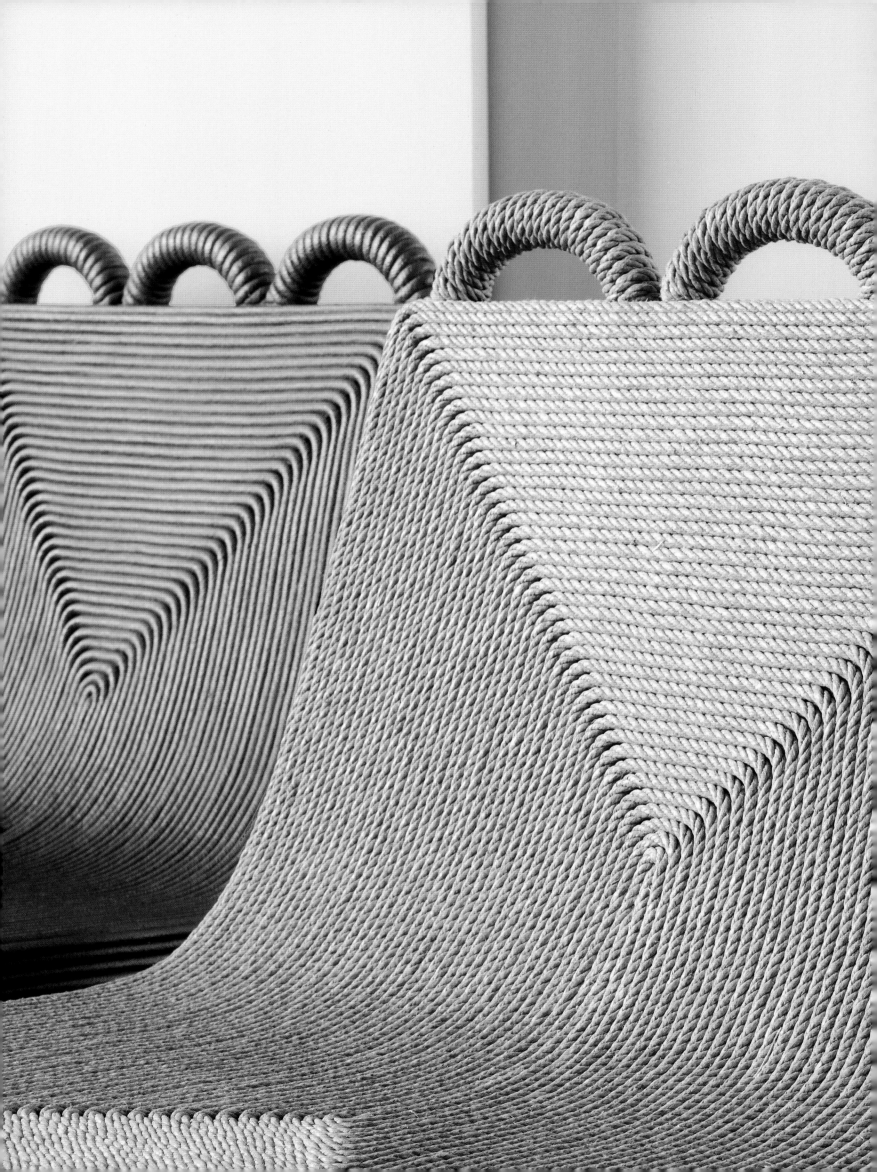

The Art of Basket Weaving

Mary A. Jackson

My mother and grandmother taught me traditional basket design, which emphasized small pieces with handles for utilitarian use. They trained me in the skills brought here by their West African ancestors, who came as slaves. I decided in my early twenties that I would make designs that no one had ever done before in this tradition.

The art form is native to the Charleston area, and this is the only place in the United States where these baskets are made. They have always been crafted from the sea grasses that grow in the wetlands of coastal South Carolina. As men do in this community, my husband goes out and harvests the grasses when they're green. The grasses are then laid in the sun to dry. As they dry, they develop certain colors.

I have not changed any of the materials of the tradition, but I am using them in a different way to give my baskets a more modern look. The traditional designs are smaller in size for holding bread and rolls, or to be used as sewing baskets. Some of my new ideas—which are considered modern designs—take inspiration from these forms.

The particular basket shown on the following pages is a form that I have come up with on my own and made several times. It evolved from a classic rice basket, which was a flat, disk-like tray with a little raised edge that was popular for cleaning rice on the plantation. This basket, the one with the grass flowing, is a version of that. Nancy and Jim came with the idea of wanting to make this design bigger than I'd ever done before—much bigger. The smaller version, which they own as well, is twenty-two inches in diameter. This big basket is approximately forty-two inches in diameter.

That scale became challenging to execute, not only because I had never done anything that large before, but also because at that scale it becomes very difficult to control the shape and to keep everything lined up so that it comes out to be a wonderful art piece. I doubt if I'll ever do anything that big again. It was made exclusively for them, for this particular house.

To make something on that scale was very, very difficult to do. But it is always my challenge to do something different, something new, something I have never done before. Several times I went with my husband to see the space where it was going to be, and to get the feel of the home. Most of my pieces take from three to eight weeks to complete. This one took about three years, from start to finish. I had time to work on it, because Nancy and Jim were building the house. It was completed for the opening, and I think it is one of the most beautiful baskets I have made.

In this basketry tradition, every hand makes a different stitch. My work identifies me, as does the technique I use, which no one else is doing. My hand and my technique are different from my mother's and from my grandmother's. They made beautiful traditional baskets. The handwork was pretty. But it was different from the others and from mine. That is true throughout the community. I am part of that tradition. When my daughter was a little girl, I passed it on to her. I am now teaching her daughter, who is in high school. Her interest is to carry it on one day.

I am honored to have my work in Nancy and Jim's art collection and excited to have done this special piece exclusively for them for this beautiful house. It was well worth the challenge.

PREVIOUS PAGES: Lofty vaulted ceilings with large windows allow expansive, uninterrupted views of the marshland. I purposefully designed the kitchen to be clutter-free and to bring the natural surroundings to the fore. OPPOSITE AND ABOVE: Creatures large and small are able and willing to serve, but can be concealed behind sliding doors when off-duty.

OPPOSITE: Dried and twisted manzanita branches in Robert Kuo's bronze planters provide a touch of the outdoors in a windowless powder room. A mirror and vanity of custom lacquered wood coupled with a small recessed sink create interest through contrast of scale. OVERLEAF: In the master bedroom, a nine-foot-high custom wood bed made by Bud Galland, a rope sculpture, and side tables by Christian Astuguevieille create a powerfully scaled composition rounded out by Robert Kuo's large urns and bowls. PAGES 272-273: Grand proportion and scale are also apparent in these views of the master bedroom. A sofa by Christian Astuguevieille, an armoire by Bud Galland, and floor urns by Robert Kuo extend the continuity of craft and craftsmanship.

OPPOSITE AND OVERLEAF: Smooth, white surfaces contrast hugely with the large cleft stone pavers that face the walls and cover the floor of this bath. Hammered coppered toads travel to and fro, perhaps in search of a drop to drink.

OPPOSITE AND ABOVE: This cream and white bedroom is a pale retreat from the bright sunny beach. Ceiling tracks concealed in the bed cornice allow sheer linen draperies to be moved at whim.

RIGHT: On a bedside table, Robert Kuo's lacquered pieces add decorative accent without visual intrusion.
OVERLEAF: To add a touch of three-dimensional whimsy, I mounted Kuo's cream-lacquered spheres on the wall.

Drum tables with removable lids and wall-mounted cabinets put an emphasis on function. The glass vases by Robert Kuo contribute a spot of color.

ABOVE AND OPPOSITE: Radishes and rabbits: Rabbits for children and radishes for
rabbits make everyone happy. OVERLEAF: A partially sunken tub provides easy
bathing in this children's bathroom.

In this children's bedroom, a flock of sheep happily graze amid the dots.

ABOVE: Scarab knobs offer good tidings to guests. OPPOSITE: Through the bedroom window, masses of sweet grass can be seen swaying gently in the ocean breeze. Inside is a tour de force of woven sweet grass by Mary Jackson.

Acknowledgments

With great appreciation to all my clients, it has been a privilege to share the design adventure with you over the years. With special gratitude to the Rollins families, thank you for the honor of allowing me to grow with you through the generations. To the Cheney family, you have my enduring gratitude for the trust you place in me.

I am privileged to have met two people who have been extraordinarily instrumental in my life. Deanne Deavours Levison, you taught me how to use my eyes. For this, and for so much else, I am enduringly grateful. Dara Caponigro, you have championed me and my work so steadfastly that it humbles me. You are a true friend and a kindred spirit.

My heartfelt thanks to all the editors over the years who have included me in the pages of their magazines and books. Particular appreciation goes to *House Beautiful*, which launched my career, and to *Veranda*, which has always supported me. To Lisa Newsom, the founder of *Veranda* and its original editor-in-chief, you have my enduring respect and gratitude for the inspiration you have provided to me and to interior designers everywhere.

To everyone at Rizzoli, and in particular Charles Miers, thank you for shepherding this book from conception to completion. To Kathleen Jayes, my editor, I am grateful for your support and belief in my work.

Jill Cohen, you are the ultimate professional. Thank you for convincing me that I could do a book that was true to my vision, and for assembling the team that has helped me make that book a reality.

To the talented Doug Turshen, and to his associate Steve Turner, endless thanks for your tireless patience and extraordinary good humor in designing and redesigning this book until it fully reflected me and my aesthetic to the last detail. Phew!

To the exceptional photographer Simon Upton, I cannot express the extent of my thanks for the pleasure it has been to work with you. With your boundless energy and optimism, you have captured my vision in a clear and insightful way. To Isabel Para, Simon's assistant, my gratitude for your constancy and vigilance.

For the other greatly talented photographers who have documented my work for publication over the years, and whose photographs color these pages, I feel privileged to know you. Thank you Jack Winston, Jonn Coolidge, William Waldron, Thibault Jeanson, Melanie Acevedo, and Emily Jenkins Followill.

To Judith Nasatir, I am grateful for your patience and your unwavering belief that we could—and would—find my voice in just the right words. This was not always an easy task, but it was a worthy process.

I am honored to have worked with many talented architects over the years: James Choate of Surber Barber Choate and Hertlein Architects, P.C.; Norman Davenport Askins Architect; Marvin Herman and Associates; Pak Heydt and Associates; and Bobby McAlpine of McAlpine Tankersley Architecture. All of you have given me the gift of collaboration, which has made our projects together more than they would have been otherwise.

I am endlessly grateful to the craftspeople and artisans whose unique talents contribute so much to the rooms I envision. Mary Jackson, you are truly singular as an artist and deeply valued as a friend. Robert Kuo, I cannot thank you enough for your multi-faceted talents and the whimsy and brio that your sculptures bring to each environment where they live. Jill Biskin, your remarkable skills as a fine artist, your eye for color, and your true passion for collaboration elevate the everyday to the exceptional. Doug Funkhouser, you are a visual artist par excellence. Linda Ridings Rubino, it was gift to know you and embark on the adventure of artistic collaboration. As well, working in metal with Andrew T Crawford Ironworks was creatively inspiring. Kevin Reilly, the lighting you have created for me absolutely illuminates my clients' worlds and my own. Bud Galland of Premier Woodworks, I am constantly amazed by your ability to fit together seamlessly the pieces of every design puzzle I generate.

There are three Atlanta galleries that I return to again and again for fine art photography, contemporary craft pieces, and superb framing: Jackson Fine Art, The Signature Shop and Gallery, and Myott Studio.

The design of a home is one thing, building it to realize its intended beauty is another. Thank you to Bonner Custom Homes, Russ Cooper Associates Inc., Gary Calicchia of Calicchia Construction Company, Larry Head and Associates, and Rafael Galeano of Ragsyl Painting Services Llc. for your immeasurable contributions in that regard. With thanks to Karl Beckwith Smith and Victor Scott Vaughn, whose remarkable artistry added immeasurable creative dimensions to our Kiawah house.

No interior comes into being without the help of skilled professional workrooms. I have had the pleasure of collaborating with a number of them around the country that are as demanding of excellence as I am. My thanks to William Pitt Curtain Makers, R. Hopkins and Co., Zirlin Interiors, Judy Pratt and Associates, and Marteca Landers for your dedication to your craft. For comfort, I rely on Craig Swenson Inc. and Tecnosedia, superb upholstery workrooms. Great thanks to the professionals in the showrooms at the Atlanta Decorative Arts Center (ADAC)—many of whom have become friends—for their expertise in helping our office complete our projects.

Landscape design and its implementation are arts unto themselves, and ones that reveal their true identities only over time. To William T. Smith and Associates, my deepest thanks for your inspired sense of natural beauty, as shaped by the hand of man. To Clint Weimann of Good Natured Gardening and Spann Landscape Inc., you have my appreciation for your botanical know-how and your ability to tend and nurture a garden to its finest form.

I could not achieve what I need to accomplish without the help of Janet Ann Ford, first and foremost, who is instrumental in all facets of my office and to whom I give heartfelt thanks. To Lori Roth, Beth Kelley, Petti Lighthart, Sheryl Grayson, and Pat Hornsby, so many thanks to all of you. Anne Stiles Quatrano and Susan Massar with John Warner and Randy Minter, your beautiful food and flowers enhance our palates and our views.

In memory of Joye Hirsch, who is often in my thoughts.

Should I have inadvertently neglected to mention any of my many colleagues and collaborators over the years, please know that you have my sincere appreciation.

Thanks to my parents, who gave me a firm grounding in the joys of hard work and the importance of high standards. I wish you were here now to see this book, and your great-grandchildren. To my husband, who is everything to me. For my amazingly gifted children, who have endured my need to constantly rearrange the furniture, and for our grandchildren, you are the wondrous future. Thank you for the glorious life journey we share. It is all of you who make my efforts worthwhile.

First published in the United States of America in 2014
by Rizzoli International Publications, Inc.
300 Park Avenue South
New York, NY 10010
www.rizzoliusa.com

All photography by Simon Upton except:
Melanie Acevedo: page 40
Jonn Coolidge: pages 22/23, 25, 28, 31, 58/59, 60, 74/75, 189, 191, 192/193, 194, 195, 197, 198/199, 201
Emily Followill: page 20
Thibault Jeanson: pages 72/73
Photograph by Jack Winston. Reprinted by permission of House Beautiful, 1993: pages 62/63, 70
William Waldron: pages 176/177, 178/179, 180/181, 182/183, 184/185, 186, 187

Design by Doug Turshen with Steve Turner

2020 2021 / 15 14

Distributed in the U.S. trade by Random House, New York

Printed in China

ISBN-13: 978-0-8478-4361-9

Library of Congress Catalog Control Number: 2014938613